Seeing in the Dark

Explorer Challenge

Find out what is sniffing
this mushroom ...

OXFORD
UNIVERSITY PRESS

Gran had a bed of strawberries. The strawberries were ready to pick.

"But it's almost bedtime," said Gran. "Let's pick them tomorrow."

Biff and Chip liked staying with Gran. She always told them funny bedtime stories.

Next morning, Gran gave the children a
big bowl. It was time to pick the strawberries.
"We can make jam with some of them,"
said Gran.

In the night something sad had happened.
The strawberry bed was a mess.

"Oh no!" said Biff. "Something has been
eating the strawberries!"

Another odd thing had happened. Three
big holes had been dug in Gran's lawn.
   "I wonder what has done this," said Chip.
"What has dug up the lawn?"

Gran looked at the wall. Part of it had
fallen down.
"I think I know," said Gran.

Gran went on the Internet and placed an order.
"What are you doing, Gran?" asked Chip.
"You'll see," said Gran.

They went outside.

"Now help me fill in the holes in my lawn," said Gran. "Then we'll go and get some strawberries from the shop."

Later, a box arrived at Gran's cottage.
"What's in it, Gran?" asked Biff.
"You'll see," said Gran.

When it was dark, Gran opened the box.
"These are night-vision binoculars," she said.

"Wow!" said Chip. "These night-vision binoculars are fantastic. We can see things in the dark."

That night, Gran woke up the children.
"Come and see this," she said.

A badger was digging in Gran's lawn.
"It's digging for worms and grubs," said
Gran.

The badger went across to Gran's apple tree.
"It has sniffed out a fallen apple," said Gran.
"Now we know what ate the strawberries,"
said Chip.

The next morning Gran took Biff and Chip to
the woods. They came to a hole by a fallen tree.
"This hole must be the badger's sett," said Gran.

She put down a few apples on the bank.
"These are for the badger," she said.

"The badger got in through the broken wall," said Gran. "I like badgers, but I don't want them in my garden."

"You are good at drawing, Chip," said Biff. "Let's play a trick on Gran. Can you make two masks?"

The children stayed awake until it was dark. Then they went outside.

"Get your night-vision binoculars, Gran," called Chip.

"My goodness!" said Gran. "Two more badgers on my lawn. Would you like worms for supper?"

Retell the Story

Look at the pictures and retell the story in your own words.

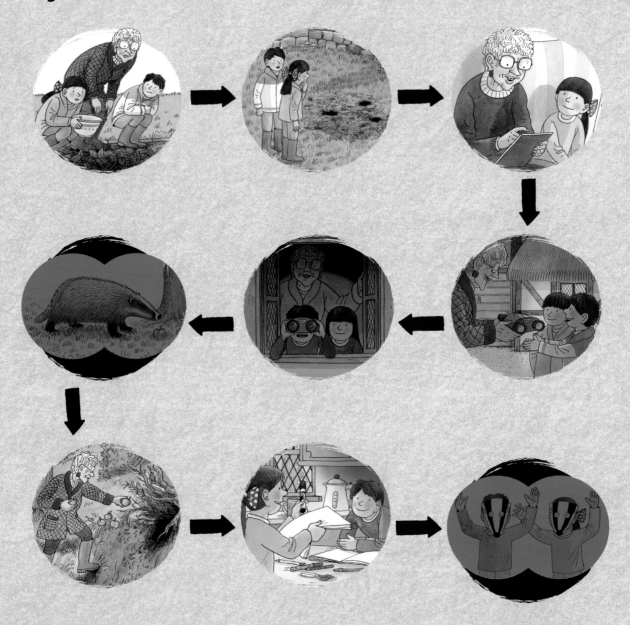

Look Back, Explorers

Which two items of fruit did the badger eat?

What was Gran going to make with the strawberries?

Why did Gran ask Biff and Chip if they would like worms for supper?

The badger *sniffed* out an apple. Can you think of other words to describe using your sense of smell or your sense of sight?

Did you find out what was sniffing this mushroom?

What's Next, Explorers?

Now that you've read about Biff and Chip using night-vision binoculars to see in the dark, find out about all the senses ...

Super
Senses

Anita Ganeri

Series created by Roderick Hunt and Alex Brychta

OXFORD

Explorer Challenge
for *Super Senses*

Find out what this tongue is used for ...